09

J

Franklin D. Roosevelt

A LEADER IN TROUBLED TIMES

By the Editors of TIME FOR KIDS
WITH JEREMY CAPLAN

HarperCollins*Publishers*

About the Author: Jeremy Caplan, a former editor at TIME FOR KIDS®, is currently a reporter for TIME magazine. A graduate of the Woodrow Wilson School at Princeton University, he is an avid violinist, athlete, and cook. The author lives in New York City.

Library of Congress Cataloging-in-Publication Data is available.
ISBN-10: 0-06-057615-4 (pbk.) — ISBN-10: 0-06-057616-2 (trade)
ISBN-13: 978-0-06-057615-8 (pbk.) — ISBN-13: 978-0-06-057616-5 (trade)

1 2 3 4 5 6 7 8 9 10
First Edition

Photography and Illustration Credits:
Cover: Bettmann–Corbis; cover inset: Time Life Pictures–Getty Images; cover flap: Atlanta Historical Society; title page: Corbis; contents page: Bettmann–Corbis; p.iv: Time Life Pictures–Getty Images; p.2: Bettmann–Corbis; p.3: Bettmann–Corbis; p.4: AP Photo; p.5: Franklin D. Roosevelt Presidential Library & Museum; p.6: Franklin D. Roosevelt Presidential Library & Museum; p.7: Franklin D. Roosevelt Presidential Library & Museum; p.8: Franklin D. Roosevelt Presidential Library & Museum; p.9 (top): Jim McKnight–AP Photo; p.9 (bottom): Franklin D. Roosevelt Presidential Library & Museum; p.10: courtesy of Groton School; p.11: Franklin D. Roosevelt Presidential Library & Museum; p.12: Franklin D. Roosevelt Presidential Library & Museum; p.13: Franklin D. Roosevelt Presidential Library & Museum; p.14: Franklin D. Roosevelt Presidential Library & Museum; p.15: Corbis; p.16: Franklin D. Roosevelt Presidential Library & Museum; p.17: AP Photo; p.18: Legacy Historical Antiques; p.19: UPI; p.20: courtesy of FDR's Little White House, Georgia Dept. of Natural Resources; p.21: Franklin D. Roosevelt Presidential Library and Museum; p.22: AP Photo; p.23: Hulton Archive–Getty Images; p.24: Corbis; p.25: Bettmann–Corbis; p.26: Franklin D. Roosevelt Presidential Library & Museum; p.27: Time Life Pictures–Getty Images; p.28: AP Photo; p.29 (top): Corbis; p.29 (bottom): The Granger Collection; p.30: AP Photo; p.31: Bettmann–Corbis; pp. 32–33: AP Photo; p.34: Time Life Pictures–Getty Images; p.35: Hulton Archive–Getty Images; p.36 (top): Franklin D. Roosevelt Presidential Library & Museum; p.36 (bottom): Selwyn Tait–Corbis Sygma; p.37: Minnesota Historical Society–Corbis; p.38: Oscar White–Corbis; p.39: Time Life Pictures–Getty Images; p.40 (top): Time Life Pictures–Getty Images; p.40 (bottom): Time Magazine Inc.; p.41 (top): The Granger Collection; p.41 (bottom): Alex Wong–Getty Images; p.42: Seth Resnick–Corbis; p.43 (top): Swim Ink–Corbis; p.43 (bottom): Punchstock; p.44 (top): royalty-free–Getty Images; p.44 (middle): The Granger Collection; p.44 (middle): Culver Pictures; p.44 (bottom): Hulton Archive–Getty Images; back cover: Hulton Archive–Getty Images

Acknowledgments:
For TIME FOR KIDS: Editorial Director: Keith Garton; Editor: Jonathan Rosenbloom; Art Director: Rachel Smith; Designer: Jaye Medalia; Photography Editor: Sandy Perez

 Find out more at **www.timeforkids.com/bio/froosevelt**

CONTENTS

▲ FRANKLIN D. ROOSEVELT was the first President to give regular radio broadcasts.

CHAPTER 1

The First Fireside Chat

Times were tough all across America. Millions of people were out of work, businesses and banks had closed, and too many people were hungry and homeless. In Houston, Texas, Myra King Whitson and her children crowded around the radio to hear the new President speak. It was around 9 P.M. on Sunday, March 12, 1933. At first the radio crackled and hissed. Then the President's voice was clear.

> *"The only thing we have to fear is fear itself."*
>
> —FRANKLIN D. ROOSEVELT

Franklin Delano Roosevelt talked about the country's money problems. He described his hopes and plans for the nation. To Whitson, he sounded calm and thoughtful. When she was done listening, Whitson wrote her new President a letter. "Our radio seemed to

▲ **FAMILIES** gathered around radio sets to listen to Roosevelt's fireside chats.

bring you to us in person," she wrote. "There is a deep happiness—a feeling that we have a real share in our government."

Every time he spoke on the radio, Americans listened closely. They wanted to hear the President talk about the country's problems and his ideas for fixing them. Roosevelt received thousands of letters after his first "fireside chat." Ordinary citizens—adults and children— wrote to Roosevelt with suggestions on how to help the nation overcome its problems.

During some of the saddest days in American history, President Roosevelt offered comfort with his hopeful words. He reminded people that they had the strength to carry on when things weren't going well. He encouraged them to keep trying.

Roosevelt had promised to find a job for every American who wanted to work. He also wanted to help people enjoy life. "Happiness lies not in the mere possession of money," he said. To Roosevelt, being happy meant enjoying nature, reading books, learning new things, and laughing with friends.

This is the story of Franklin Delano Roosevelt, a President who helped many Americans and who brightened some of the nation's darkest times.

▲ MILLIONS of Americans hoped Roosevelt would create jobs and improve their lives.

CHAPTER 2

Franklin's Early Years

Franklin Delano Roosevelt was born on January 30, 1882. He was a big baby, with bright, blond hair. His mother, Sara, had many servants, but she loved Franklin so much that she fed, bathed, and dressed him herself every morning. He was her only child.

Sara was twenty-eight when Franklin was born. James, Franklin's father, was fifty-four. He was a businessman and spent much of his time taking care of the family's land

◄ **SARA ROOSEVELT** took excellent care of her only child.

▲ FRANKLIN spent a lot of time with his father, whom he called Popsy.

in Hyde Park, New York. The Roosevelts lived there in a huge home called Springwood, which overlooked the Hudson River. They also had a home in New York City, where they spent part of the year.

The Roosevelt family had been in America for a long time. Sara's ancestors had arrived at Plymouth Colony in Massachusetts in 1621. James's relatives had also been in America for generations. Franklin was born into a wealthy family with a proud history.

▲ FRANKLIN (far left) often played with his cousins—and a pet goat!

A Life of Luxury

Instead of going to elementary school, Franklin learned at home. Sara taught him how to read and write. Then, from age six on, Franklin studied with private tutors. They taught him Latin, German, and French. He also studied math, science, geography, and history. Franklin learned about America's past—its great leaders and its struggles. His tutors said he was smart and asked good questions.

Franklin worked hard, but he also had a lot of time for play. However, his parents didn't let him spend much time with children from the neighborhood. His overprotective mother worried he would learn bad habits from local kids. Instead, Franklin played alone or with his many cousins. He and his father were also close friends. James taught his son how to ice-skate, swim, and ride a horse. He also shared his love of nature with Franklin. The two often rode their horses or hiked through the woods and fields surrounding their home.

James encouraged his son to collect all kinds of things. Franklin started a stamp collection when he was ten years old. He gathered birds' nests and eggs, and wrote down everything he noticed about them in a notebook. Franklin also enjoyed taking photographs with a camera his parents gave him.

◄ HOP ON!
Franklin was about six when this photo was taken. He liked to ride around the grounds of his home.

Franklin had the chance to travel with his parents. James and Sara first took Franklin to Europe when he was just three years old. When he was nine, the Roosevelts spent a summer in Germany. From a very early age, Franklin saw how people lived all over the world. He got to meet lots of interesting people, listening carefully to what they had to say. And he experienced the differences between the United States and other countries. This knowledge proved to be useful when he was President.

While Franklin's education and travels were unusual for a boy his age, he was just like most kids in other ways. Sometimes he played tricks on people or got into mischief. Once, when he was nine, he hid in a tall tree while his parents searched everywhere for him. And at times he ran away from his teachers to avoid his reading or piano lessons. Luckily Franklin knew just the right thing to say to be forgiven every time. Many years later, when he became President, he would use that charm to help win support from those who disagreed with him.

▼ SAY CHEESE! Franklin loved to take photographs.

A VISIT TO HYDE PARK

You can visit Springwood, the Roosevelt family home in Hyde Park, New York. Springwood is a National Historic Site open to visitors.

People can tour the home and see how the Roosevelt family lived. There are stables, an ice house (where food was kept cool), rose gardens, trails, and the grave site where Franklin and his wife, Eleanor, are buried. There is also the FDR Presidential Library and Museum, which has lots of exhibits about the President and his family.

Val-Kill, Eleanor's cottage, is just down the road.

For more information on Springwood and Val-Kill, go to the National Park Service website at www.nps.gov.

CHAPTER 3

Leaving Home for School

Once Franklin turned fourteen, his parents sent him to boarding school. They chose Groton, a private school for boys in Massachusetts. When he arrived at Groton, Franklin was nervous about fitting in. Most of the other students had been at the school for two years

and already knew one another. Franklin feared it would be hard to make friends.

Having studied with private tutors, Franklin was well prepared for school. He earned good grades, especially for neatness. And he was always

◄ THE GROTON CHAPEL was—and still is—a center of activity at the school.

▲ THE BOY IN THE HAT is Franklin. He is surrounded by the baseball team at Groton.

on time for class. Sometimes the other boys thought Franklin was *too* well behaved. They teased him for being such a quiet student and for not being good at baseball or football. Franklin was good at tennis, sailing, and skating, but he had never played team sports. He was put on the worst baseball and football teams in the school.

When Franklin was left off the good teams, he felt embarrassed. But he decided to find something he was good at. One day Franklin tried a Groton game called High Kick. Players would take turns jumping to kick a can hanging from the ceiling. Franklin found he could kick a can that was more than seven feet high! He was happy to win some respect at school.

While at Groton, Franklin became a skilled speaker and won many debates. With clever ideas and a strong voice, he convinced people with his words. Franklin said things he believed in and spoke from the heart.

Off to College

After graduating from Groton in 1900, Franklin went to Harvard University. His favorite subjects were history, government, and English.

But Franklin was not one of the best students in his class. Many of his professors gave him Cs. They said he should spend more time studying and less time partying.

However, one thing Franklin was very serious about was the school newspaper, *The Harvard Crimson*.

Franklin often spent whole afternoons and evenings at the paper's office. He wrote stories, edited other students' articles, and came up with new ideas for the college publication.

Franklin's friends on the staff thought he had great ways to improve the paper. They chose him as the editor during his final year. Franklin spent even more hours working on *The Harvard Crimson*. He also spent a lot of time thinking about his new love, a woman named Eleanor.

▲ FRANKLIN (in the bowtie) hung out with some college friends at his cousin's house.

CHAPTER 4

Going into Politics

Franklin first met Eleanor
Roosevelt when they were
children. They were fifth
cousins and played together
at family gatherings. When
Franklin was in his last year
at Harvard, they started
going out together regularly.
He visited her home in New
York City. Eleanor showed
him the homeless shelters
where she volunteered.
She also talked to him

▶ ELEANOR opened Franklin's eyes to
people who were less fortunate than he.

▲ KIDS AS YOUNG AS TEN worked at dangerous factory jobs.

about the unfairness of young children working long hours in noisy, poorly lighted, and dangerous factories.

Franklin was impressed by the compassion Eleanor showed to everyone, including the poor. Her kindness rubbed off on Franklin, and he began to wonder what he could do to help others.

By Thanksgiving of 1903, Franklin told his mother he wanted to marry Eleanor. At first Sara was

▲ READING WAS A FAVORITE family activity for the Roosevelts.

disappointed. She thought her son was too young to get married and that her son deserved a more beautiful and stylish wife. But Sara gradually accepted her. After all, Eleanor's uncle was President Theodore Roosevelt!

Franklin and Eleanor married on St. Patrick's Day 1905 in New York City. Franklin had just started studying at Columbia University Law School. When he finished school for the year, he and Eleanor went to Europe for a long honeymoon. In May 1906 the Roosevelts had their first child, Anna. Over the next ten years, they had five more children—one of whom died at an early age. Eleanor was a busy mother. She took care of a house full of children while Franklin was busy studying and working.

Meanwhile, Franklin finished law school and started a career as a New York City lawyer. But he found the work boring. Franklin dreamed of doing something different. Influenced by Eleanor, he wanted to do more for those who needed help.

Franklin Runs for the Senate

Franklin decided that he could do good for people by going into politics. To start his new career, in 1910, Roosevelt ran for the New York State Senate as a member of the Democratic Party. He gave ten speeches a day to voters in his Hyde Park district. Sometimes his voice would wear thin from talking so much.

At first Roosevelt was nervous about speaking to big crowds of strangers. But he soon

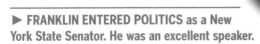
▶ FRANKLIN ENTERED POLITICS as a New York State Senator. He was an excellent speaker.

grew used to giving one speech after another. He remembered how easy it was at Groton to stand up and say what was on his mind. By the end of his campaign, Roosevelt was an excellent speaker. He criticized powerful, lazy politicians. He spoke about making New York's government work better, and the importance of preserving nature through conservation. He won the election, taking office for the first time.

Off to Washington

Roosevelt got sick with typhoid fever in 1912. Up for re-election to the New York State Senate, he didn't have the strength to campaign. But even though other people gave speeches for him, the young politician was so popular that he won easily.

Soon his thoughts turned to national politics. In 1913 he was chosen by President Woodrow Wilson to be the Assistant Secretary of the Navy in Washington, D.C. He made decisions about how the navy would prepare for the war that was about to break out—World War I.

Roosevelt did an outstanding job as naval secretary and earned the respect of other politicians. James M.

Cox, who was the Democratic Party's choice for President in 1920, asked Roosevelt to be his vice presidential running mate. The pair campaigned hard across the country but lost to Warren G. Harding and Calvin Coolidge.

About this time Franklin's relationship with Eleanor started to fade. The very busy couple weren't as close as they had been. Even though they were still married, they started to treat each other as friends and business partners rather than as husband and wife. But losing the election and struggling through marriage weren't Roosevelt's only problems.

▼ HATS OFF! James M. Cox and Franklin campaigned across the United States—but the pair lost the race.

CHAPTER 5

A Run for President

In 1921 Franklin came down with a virus that attacks the spinal cord. He was treated for polio, although some doctors today think he may have had a different illness. Soon he was paralyzed from the waist down.

Franklin worked hard to strengthen his body. He went to Warm Springs, Georgia, a place that some thought had healing waters. Franklin exercised and tried to build up his leg

◄ FRANKLIN spent time in Warm Springs, Georgia, where he relaxed, wrote, and swam.

20

▲ FRANKLIN'S DOG, FALA, and a neighbor were photographed with him. There are only a few photos of Franklin in a wheelchair.

muscles by swimming. But nothing seemed to help. He was a proud man and embarrassed that his illness kept him from walking on his own. Louis Howe, Franklin's close friend and advisor, and Eleanor helped him keep up his spirits. They encouraged him to keep fighting for the ideas he believed in. That inspired him to stay in politics.

However, his illness raised new questions. What would people think of a leader who couldn't walk on his own? Would they still vote for him? Franklin almost never allowed photos to be taken of him in his wheelchair or on crutches. He thought people might see them as a sign of weakness. Most Americans knew very little about Franklin's polio and wouldn't learn about it for years to come.

A New Job for Franklin

These difficult years didn't end Franklin's dreams of political greatness. He decided to run for governor of New York in 1928. Franklin was familiar with the state's problems and was still popular with New Yorkers. He won the election by 25,000 votes.

Even though Franklin suffered physical challenges, his spirit was as strong as ever. As governor of New

▼ FRANKLIN LIKED
to drive around New York
State and talk to citizens.

▲ **ELEANOR AND FRANKLIN** were surrounded by admirers on the campaign trail.

York, he pushed through several conservation bills and lowered taxes for farmers. After two years he was elected to another term. Then he was ready for an even bigger challenge. He decided to run for President of the United States.

Franklin knew that being President would not be an easy job. In 1929 the stock market had crashed. Businesses folded and jobs were hard to find. By 1932 twelve million Americans—about one in ten people—were out of work. Many banks had closed because

ROOSEVELT SAID IT!

"A nation that destroys its soils destroys itself. Forests are the lungs of our land, purifying the air and giving fresh strength to our people."

"A nation does not have to be cruel to be tough."

"If you treat people right they will treat you right . . . ninety percent of the time."

"Be sincere; be brief; be seated." (when giving a speech)

"There are many ways of going forward, but only one way of standing still."

"When you get to the end of your rope, tie a knot and hang on."

depositors had taken out their money. People didn't have enough to eat and worried about surviving. Many couldn't afford to pay their rent or buy medicine and winter clothing. Some were living in towns of cardboard shacks called Hoovervilles, named in anger after the current President, Herbert Hoover. The country was suffering from the Great Depression.

Franklin promised that if he became President, the government would offer more support to the poor, the homeless, and the jobless. He wanted to start up programs that would help people get back to work. In his speeches, he announced that he wanted to offer Americans a "New Deal."

▲ HOOVERVILLES, where homeless people lived, sprang up across the United States.

Some people worried that, because of his polio, Franklin wouldn't be strong enough to be President. But with Eleanor often at his side, he campaigned day after day across the country, proving he was healthy enough to be a leader. When Election Day finally arrived in November 1932, he won easily, carrying forty-two out of forty-eight states. At a celebration at Hyde Park, Franklin smiled and laughed, thanking his friends and family for helping him win. But the hardest job and the hardest times were still ahead.

"THE ONLY THING WE HAVE TO FEAR IS FEAR ITSELF--"

1933

MARCH 4, 1933

▲ ROOSEVELT'S most famous quote decorates this photo from his inauguration.

CHAPTER 6

Welcome to the White House

On March 4, 1933, Franklin Delano Roosevelt, now often known as FDR, was sworn in as President. On that day he gave a famous speech. He said, "The only thing we have to fear is fear itself." He wanted to assure people that things would soon be better. His speech lifted people's spirits.

In his first hundred days as President, FDR started to improve life for all Americans with his New Deal program. One of the first things he did was to start to repair the bank system. He temporarily shut down all the banks and then allowed only the strongest banks—those with the most money

▲ FDR LISTENED to Americans' problems as he toured the country.

and best management—to reopen. He also got a law passed that insured the money people kept in banks. This helped to build more confidence in the system.

Next FDR began to create jobs for people. The first new program he started was the Civilian Conservation Corps (CCC). The Corps hired about 250,000 people to clean up national parks and forests. Although workers earned only about one dollar a day, they had an opportunity to support their families. Other new programs helped Americans find work rebuilding cities.

Slowly the new job programs put people back to work. But the improvements took time, and many people thought FDR wasn't acting fast enough. Others were alarmed that the government was spending so much money. But with his advisors helping him make decisions, FDR ignored critics and kept creating jobs. He refused to let people who didn't like his ideas stop him from trying to help the poorest Americans.

▲ THIS EDITORIAL CARTOON pokes fun at "alphabet" programs FDR started.

While her husband was busy being President, Eleanor was busy as First Lady. She traveled everywhere, visiting the poor and the sick. Eleanor wanted to make the country a safer, healthier place for everyone. She always reminded her husband about the importance of taking care of the nation's people.

On the Road to Recovery

When it came time for FDR to run for re-election in 1936, the United States was getting over some of its worst problems. The number of unemployed people had dropped. Farmers were earning more for their crops. Companies were making more money. Some people still didn't like FDR's policies. In 1935 he had convinced Congress to raise the taxes of the wealthiest

◀ REST EASY! A woman shows off her Social Security card—the result of one of FDR's greatest programs.

Americans and companies. This helped pay for more job-creating programs and insurance plans for the poor. Many wealthy people didn't like paying more money to the government. But since most citizens supported the New Deal, FDR remained popular.

One of FDR's most important new programs was the Social Security System. It made sure that retired people would have an income after they stopped working. Social Security is still helping people today.

In the 1936 election, FDR won all but two states—Vermont and Maine. The President once again celebrated at his Hyde Park home after his victory.

MYSTERY PEOPLE

☛ **CLUE 1:** In 1939 this couple became the first British monarchs to ever visit the United States. FDR had invited them so that Britain and the United States would stay good friends.

☛ **CLUE 2:** The king and queen were served a picnic lunch of hot dogs at Hyde Park.

☛ **CLUE 3:** Their daughter is Queen Elizabeth II.

Who are they?

ANSWER: KING GEORGE VI AND QUEEN ELIZABETH

CHAPTER 7

America Goes to War

Soon after the 1936 election, FDR had a new set of problems. In Germany Adolf Hitler and his Nazi party were gaining power and threatening neighboring countries. Japan was moving against Korea and China. When Germany invaded Poland in 1939, many European and Asian nations went to war. World War II was under way.

▶ THE ATTACK ON PEARL HARBOR led to America's entry into World War II.

At first FDR said the United States would be better off staying out of the war. But then on December 7, 1941, Japan launched a surprise attack on Pearl Harbor, the American naval base in Hawaii. Almost 2,400 people were killed. Much of the Pacific fleet—twenty-one naval vessels—was sunk or damaged, and three hundred planes were destroyed. It was a painful day for the United States.

When the President was told of the attack, he knew the United States must fight back. The next day he spoke before Congress and asked the lawmakers to declare

▲ **THE PRESIDENT SIGNS** a Declaration of War as his aides look on.

war. The nation listened to FDR's speech on the radio as he announced that December 7 was "a date that would live in infamy." The American public agreed with the President, and Congress voted to go to war.

FDR, who had been elected for a record third time in 1940, met with Britain's Prime Minister, Winston Churchill, and the Soviet Premier, Joseph Stalin. They planned careful strategies for fighting the war. Roosevelt also worked with his advisors at home to find ways to attack Germany and Japan where they were weakest. Hundreds of thousands of soldiers from many countries died as fighting carried on.

Roosevelt was a strong, confident leader. In his fireside chats, he used his steady speaking voice to urge the country to be patient and proud—and to remain hopeful. The American people did all they could to help the war effort. They used less butter, sugar, and other goods so the U.S. could send them to soldiers overseas. Many women went to work because the men were fighting. The war created jobs and helped the economy as the nation did all it could to produce materials to win the fight.

▼ CHURCHILL, FDR, AND STALIN met several times during the war to plan strategies.

LIFE ON THE HOME FRONT

While soldiers were fighting overseas during World War II, Americans at home were being asked to sacrifice for the war effort. In 1942 the government gave each citizen (including kids) a book of ration coupons. These coupons were used to help buy scarce items such as sugar, butter, coffee, and beef. Homemakers had to put all their family's stamps together to plan meals. In addition, gasoline, rubber, and many metals were rationed so they could be used for war materials. People also recycled their metal and rubber scrap for the government.

During the war, Victory gardens sprang up across the

In 1944, as the war raged on in Europe and Asia, FDR decided to run again for President. He felt the nation needed his leadership despite the fact that he was in poor health. Again he won the election easily. Americans admired him and didn't want to change Presidents in wartime. During the inauguration ceremony marking the start of his fourth term, FDR's grandchildren joined him. This would be the last time the whole family would celebrate his victories.

country. The government encouraged people to grow fresh vegetables in their backyards, empty lots, and on school playgrounds as part of a food-growing plan. Soon six million Americans were raising vegetables.

Many schools taught students how to plant vegetables so they could help out in the Victory gardens. And every morning kids said the Pledge of Allegiance as a sign

▶ POSTERS reminded people to grow veggies.

of patriotism. World maps hung in classrooms as teachers and students followed the war. Faraway places that were the scenes of huge battles, such as Iwojima and Guadalcanal in the Pacific, became familiar names.

The war brought Americans closer together to help their country. It was a time of sacrifice by soldiers in battle as well as by citizens at home.

◀ AMERICANS HAD RATION BOOKS for everything—from food to gasoline.

WAR GARDENS FOR VICTORY
GROW VITAMINS AT YOUR KITCHEN DOOR

CHAPTER 8

A Sad Farewell

In 1945 FDR's health gradually got worse as his responsibilities got harder and harder because of the war. On April 12, 1945, he said to an assistant, "I have a terrific headache." Then he died suddenly in Warm Springs, Georgia. Vice President Harry S. Truman became the nation's thirty-third President.

A train carried FDR's body along the east coast to the funeral in Washington. Tens of thousands of people lined up to watch

◀ VICE PRESIDENT Harry S. Truman became President when FDR died.

38

▲ FDR'S FLAG-COVERED COFFIN traveled through the streets of Washington, D.C.

the train pass. Silently they honored their beloved leader. Thousands more people lined the streets of Washington, D.C., as FDR's casket was taken from Union Station.

A simple service took place in the White House. Diplomats from many countries came to pay their respects. Winston Churchill, Roosevelt's close friend and ally in the war, said that he felt he had "suffered a physical blow" and broke down in tears as he told the British people about the President's death. Through it all, Eleanor was calm. After the funeral Franklin was buried in the peaceful garden of his family home in Hyde Park.

A FINE FALA

No presidential pet is more famous than Fala, Roosevelt's Scottish terrier.

Fala went everywhere with the President. The dog slept in a chair by Roosevelt's bed.

Fred D. Fair, a butler who worked for Roosevelt, remembers what life with Fala was like:

"Before the President's meal, I would fix Fala's food. But you couldn't serve Fala yourself. You handed it to the President, and he'd feed Fala out of his hand. Many times, I remember... important folks waiting for their supper until Mr. Roosevelt finished feeding Fala."

Fala is buried in Hyde Park a few yards from Franklin Roosevelt.

Americans mourned the death of a man who had been President for a history-making twelve years. He had led the nation through some of its darkest days of battle and its weakest moments of poverty.

In August 1945 the United States dropped two atomic bombs on Japan.

▼ ROOSEVELT appeared on eight covers of TIME magazine.

6c

FRANKLIN D. ROOSEVELT
U.S. POSTAGE

◀ A UNITED STATES postage stamp was designed and printed in FDR's memory.

More than two hundred thousand people were killed. The Japanese government surrendered, and World War II finally came to an end.

Roosevelt didn't get to see his country in victory. Yet his guidance, strong leadership, and confident words inspired others both at home and overseas. He had helped the country move toward prosperity and peace. Roosevelt's job programs gave millions of Americans dignity and pride. He turned a nation that was afraid into a nation that was hopeful and optimistic about the future. For that, he will always be remembered as one of the greatest American Presidents.

▶ THIS STATUE OF FDR in a wheelchair is at the Roosevelt Memorial in Washington, D.C.

Talking About Franklin

▲ Doris Kearns Goodwin

TIME reporter and author Jeremy Caplan spoke with Doris Kearns Goodwin about FDR. Goodwin, a historian, often writes about the U.S. Presidents.

Q. *How did FDR change the role of the President?*

A. He expanded the office, making it the center of action in a way it had not been for years. Citizens felt personally connected to him. His fireside chats were so popular that they drew audiences comparable to World Series or Superbowl games today.

Q. *What are FDR's greatest achievements?*

A. He led the American people through the two greatest crises in the twentieth century—the Great

◀ **TODAY'S CLOSE TIES** between Britain and the United States have their roots in Roosevelt's actions during World War II.

Depression and World War II. He and America's allies saved freedom and democracy.

Q. *Why did FDR care so much about the poor, having grown up wealthy?*

A. FDR had very little contact with poor people as a child. But the suffering he went through when polio left him paralyzed from the waist down gave him a great sympathy with others. Then, coming into office during the Great Depression, when so many millions were poor, he wanted to do all he could to help make things better. Also, Eleanor told him stories of average Americans, helping him understand their needs.

▶ RETIRED PEOPLE can enjoy their lives more, thanks to Social Security.

Franklin D. Roosevelt's
Key Dates

1882	Born on January 30, in Hyde Park, New York
1905	Marries his fifth cousin, Eleanor Roosevelt
1910	Wins seat in New York State Senate
1913	Named Assistant Secretary of the Navy
1921	Diagnosed with polio
1928	Elected governor of New York
1932	Elected President
1941	Asks Congress to declare war on Germany and Japan
1945	Dies on April 12, in Warm Springs, Georgia

1888 The ballpoint pen is invented.

1927 The first feature-length talking movie is made.

1936 The Spanish Civil War begins.

44